BIGGEST NAMES IN SPORTS
LEWIS HAMILTON
AUTO RACING STAR

by Harold P. Cain

FOCUS
READERS.
NAVIGATOR

WWW.FOCUSREADERS.COM

Focus Readers is distributed by North Star Editions:
sales@northstareditions.com | 888-417-0195

Produced for Focus Readers by Red Line Editorial.

Photographs ©: James Gasperotti/ZUMA Press Wire/Cal Sport Media/AP Images, cover, 1; Hoch Zwei/Picture Alliance/DPA/AP Images, 4–5, 7; Lars Baron/Getty Pool/AP Images, 9; Philip Brown/Popperfoto/Getty Images, 10–11; Shutterstock Images, 13; Eric Vargiolu/ DPPI/Icon SMI/Newscom, 15; Frank Augstein/AP Images, 16–17; Andre Penner/AP Images, 19; Photo 4/La Presse/Icon Sportswire, 21; HZ/Pixathlon/SIPA/AP Images, 22–23; Miguel Morenatti/AP Images, 25; Francisco Seco/Pool/AP Images, 27; Red Line Editorial, 29

Library of Congress Cataloging-in-Publication Data
Names: Cain, Harold P., author.
Title: Lewis Hamilton : auto racing star / by Harold P. Cain.
Description: Lake Elmo, MN : Focus Readers, [2023] | Series: Biggest names in sports | Includes index. | Audience: Grades: 4-6
Identifiers: LCCN 2022010421 (print) | LCCN 2022010422 (ebook) | ISBN 9781637392553 (hardcover) | ISBN 9781637393079 (paperback) | ISBN 9781637394083 (pdf) | ISBN 9781637393598 (ebook)
Subjects: LCSH: Hamilton, Lewis, 1985---Juvenile literature. | Automobile racing drivers--Great Britain--Biography--Juvenile literature. | Athletes, Black--Great Britain--Biography--Juvenile literature. | Formula One automobiles--Juvenile literature.
Classification: LCC GV1032.H33 C35 2023 (print) | LCC GV1032.H33 (ebook) | DDC 796.72092 [B]--dc23/eng/20220405
LC record available at https://lccn.loc.gov/2022010421
LC ebook record available at https://lccn.loc.gov/2022010422

Printed in the United States of America
Mankato, MN
082022

ABOUT THE AUTHOR

Harold P. Cain is a retired English teacher and lifelong sports fan originally from Rockford, Illinois. He and his wife now live in Cathedral City, California, where they enjoy hiking, golf, and spending time with their daughter and three grandchildren in Los Angeles.

TABLE OF CONTENTS

CHAPTER 1

THE COMEBACK

Lewis Hamilton gripped the steering wheel. The 2021 São Paulo **Grand Prix** was about to begin in Brazil. One by one, five red lights came on above the field of 20 cars. Then the lights went out, meaning the race could begin. Hamilton sped off, hoping to make up some ground.

Lewis Hamilton (front) competes in the 2021 São Paulo Grand Prix.

Hamilton had started the race in 10th place. He usually started much farther up. In fact, Hamilton had set the fastest **qualifying** time for the race. But he received a penalty. A part on his car didn't conform to the rules. So, he had to start farther back.

SPRINTING AHEAD

Hamilton's race in Brazil got off to a rough start. His penalty in the qualifying race meant he had to start the sprint race in last place. The sprint race would set the field for the main race. Hamilton fought his way up to fifth place. But then his team had to replace his engine. That meant another penalty. Hamilton wound up starting in 10th for the main race.

Hamilton (left) turns a tight corner at the 2021 São Paulo Grand Prix.

Going into the race, Hamilton was second in the Formula 1 (F1) world championship. There were just three races left in the season. Hamilton needed a strong finish. The better he finished, the more points he would earn toward the championship. Meanwhile, Max Verstappen was first in the world championship. He started the race in second.

Hamilton had 71 laps to catch up. And he got moving quickly. After two laps, he'd already made it up to fifth place. By lap 48, Hamilton was in second, right behind Verstappen. But Verstappen would be the hardest car to pass of all.

Going into Turn 4, Hamilton tried to make his move. However, Verstappen blocked and forced Hamilton off the track. Eleven laps later, Hamilton tried again. This time, he passed Verstappen before they even got to the turn. Hamilton then pulled away from his **rival** and won the race by 10 seconds.

Hamilton celebrates his victory at the 2021 São Paulo Grand Prix.

Hamilton called São Paulo the toughest weekend of his racing career. He did just what he had to do. He was now in position to win a championship. It was another memorable moment for one of the greatest racers in F1 history.

CHAPTER 2

KART KID

Lewis Hamilton was born on January 7, 1985. He grew up in a town near London, England. Lewis's parents got divorced when he was two years old. After that, he lived with his mother.

Lewis's mother was white. His father was Black. Being biracial, Lewis experienced some **racism** and bullying

Ten-year-old Lewis Hamilton prepares for a go-kart race in 1995.

11

growing up. He started practicing karate to defend himself. Lewis also enjoyed playing soccer. But his main passion was racing.

At the age of 10, Lewis started living with his father. By then, Lewis had begun racing **go-karts**. And in 1995, he became the youngest national champion in history. His father worked up to three jobs to support his son's dream.

Later in 1995, Lewis met Ron Dennis at an awards ceremony. Dennis was in charge of the McLaren Formula 1 team. Ten-year-old Lewis said he wanted to race for McLaren someday. Dennis said to call him in nine years.

Many F1 drivers start their careers racing go-karts.

It took only three years. And it was Dennis who called the Hamilton family. He wanted Lewis to join McLaren's driver development program. The program would pay for Lewis's training. And if he was good enough, he would eventually have a shot to race in F1.

By 2000, Lewis was the karting champion of Europe. The next year, Lewis got to drive in a special kart race with F1 champion Michael Schumacher. Schumacher believed Lewis was good enough to make it to F1.

After winning eight kart titles, Lewis moved on to **open-wheel** race cars.

NICOLAS HAMILTON

Lewis grew up with his half brother, Nicolas, when he moved in with his father. Nicolas was born with a muscle disorder called cerebral palsy. Doctors believed Nicolas would never walk. But Nicolas proved them wrong. He did more than walk. He also became a racing driver just like Lewis. Lewis has called Nicolas an inspiration in his career.

Hamilton drives an open-wheel car during a 2006 race in Germany.

These cars are more like F1 cars. Lewis proved he was ready for the challenge. He won three titles over the next five years. McLaren had seen enough. They promoted Lewis to F1 for the 2007 season.

CHAPTER 3

STARTING FROM THE TOP

Nobody knew whether 22-year-old Lewis Hamilton could succeed in Formula 1. Almost immediately, Hamilton showed he could. He scored his first win in just his sixth race. Hamilton was even faster than his teammate, Fernando Alonso. Alonso was a two-time world

Lewis Hamilton (left) and Fernando Alonso pose for a photo before the 2007 season.

champion. Hamilton and Alonso quickly developed a heated rivalry.

Going into the last race of the 2007 season, Hamilton led the world championship. However, he fell behind in the race. At one point, he was in 18th place. He fought back to seventh. But it wasn't enough. Hamilton lost the championship by a single point.

Alonso left McLaren in 2008. That made Hamilton the team's top driver. He showed that 2007 had been no **fluke**. Hamilton won five races in 2008. And once again, he went into the final race with a shot at the title. In the last turn, Hamilton made a pass and moved into

Hamilton races toward an F1 championship at the 2008 Brazilian Grand Prix.

fifth place. That gave him enough points to make him world champion. He was the youngest driver in history to earn the title.

Not everyone was a fan of Hamilton. Some other drivers felt he was too **aggressive** and unsafe. However, pushing the limits was what made Hamilton great.

His teammates drove very similar cars to his. But Hamilton was usually faster. He had a talent for finding the best line around the track.

Hamilton remained one of the best drivers in F1. But he couldn't quite get back to his championship form. Over the

RACING AGAINST RACISM

Hamilton was the first Black racer in F1 history. Throughout his career, he has dealt with racism from some fans. In 2008, F1 launched its "Racing Against Racism" campaign. It set consequences for fans who engaged in racism at races. Despite these efforts, Hamilton has continued to suffer racism, especially on social media.

Hamilton (rear) chases Michael Schumacher at the 2010 Monaco Grand Prix.

next four years, he finished no higher than fifth in the championship.

After the 2012 season, legendary driver Michael Schumacher announced his retirement. That opened up a spot on the Mercedes team. Hamilton filled the spot. It marked a turning point in his career.

CHAPTER 4

THE WORLD'S GREATEST

Hamilton's move to Mercedes was well timed. He finished fourth again in 2013. But the rules changed for 2014. The car that Mercedes designed turned out to be the fastest in the field. And Hamilton put it to good use. He won 11 of 19 races that season. Teammate Nico Rosberg won five. Their only challengers

Hamilton makes a pit stop at the 2014 Malaysian Grand Prix.

for the title were each other. Hamilton and Rosberg had been friends and rivals since they raced karts against each other. Hamilton came out on top this time.

The same was true in 2015. However, Rosberg fought back to win in 2016. The teammates had many fierce battles on the track. They were the two fastest cars out there. But Hamilton was usually the best. He made his tires last longer. He also stretched his fuel supply longer. Hamilton wasn't just fast. He was smart.

In 2017, Hamilton was better than ever. He eliminated many of his past mistakes. As a result, he earned a point in every single race. That season was the first of

Nico Rosberg (left) and Lewis Hamilton show off the new Mercedes car before the 2015 season.

four straight world championships for Hamilton.

In 2020, Hamilton passed Schumacher for the most wins in F1 history. And Hamilton's championship that year tied Schumacher for the most ever. All signs pointed to Hamilton breaking the record in 2021.

Going into the final race of 2021, Hamilton and Max Verstappen were tied for first place. The race took place in Abu Dhabi. And it came down to the final lap. Hamilton led, and Verstappen was second. But Verstappen had newer tires. That meant his car was faster. In Turn 5, Verstappen passed Hamilton. Hamilton

FIGHTING BATTLES

Hamilton took a leading role in fighting for racial equality in 2020 and 2021. Hamilton took a knee before each race to bring attention to social justice issues. F1 also invited other drivers to take part, either by kneeling or wearing shirts with anti-racism messages.

Hamilton kneels before a race to show his support for the Black Lives Matter movement.

tried to come back in Turn 9. But he didn't have the speed. Verstappen drove off with the championship.

Hamilton's record-breaking world title would have to wait. Still, there was no question where he stood. He ranked among the greatest drivers of all time.

LEWIS HAMILTON

- Height: 5 feet 9 inches (174 cm)
- Weight: 161 pounds (73 kg)
- Birth date: January 7, 1985
- Birthplace: Stevenage, England
- High school: John Henry Newman School (Stevenage, England)
- Formula 1 teams: McLaren (2007–12); Mercedes (2013–)
- Major awards: F1 World Champion (2008, 2014, 2015, 2017, 2018, 2019, 2020)

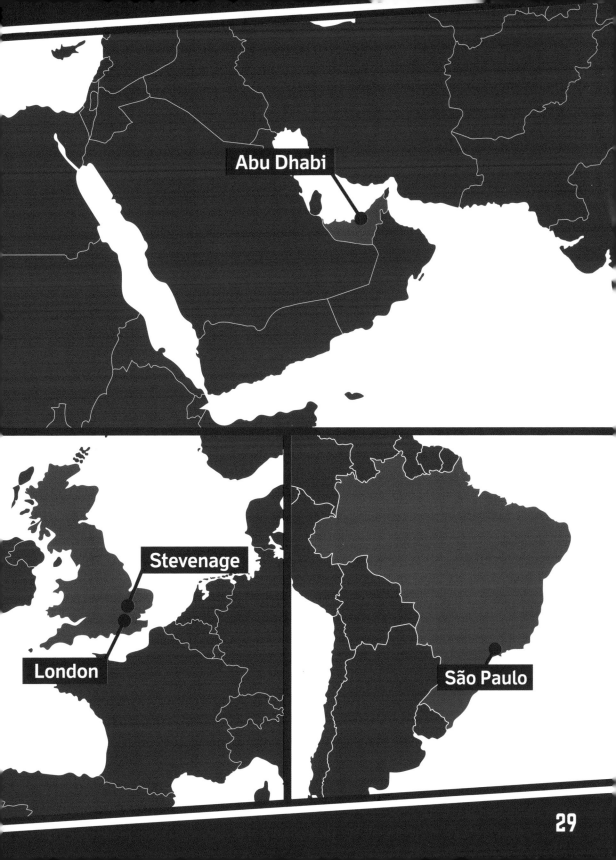

Abu Dhabi

Stevenage

London

São Paulo

FOCUS ON
LEWIS HAMILTON

Write your answers on a separate piece of paper.

1. Write a sentence that describes the main ideas from Chapter 2.

2. Would you want to be an F1 driver? Why or why not?

3. What kind of car did Hamilton start racing in?

    A. an open-wheel car

    B. a go-kart

    C. a Formula 1 car

4. Why did Ron Dennis want Lewis Hamilton to join his program?

    A. He knew Lewis would win F1 races right away.

    B. He thought Lewis could win F1 races in several years.

    C. He didn't want Lewis to pursue a career in F1 racing.

Answer key on page 32.

GLOSSARY

aggressive
Making an all-out effort to win.

fluke
An unusual event that is not expected to happen again.

go-karts
Small race cars often driven by children.

grand prix
A high-level race that is part of a series.

open-wheel
A type of race car in which the tires are not surrounded by any bodywork.

qualifying
A process to decide the starting order of a race, based on which driver has the fastest lap times.

racism
Hatred or mistreatment of people because of their skin color or ethnicity.

rival
A team or player that has an intense and ongoing competition against another team or player.

TO LEARN MORE

BOOKS

Albino, Dustin. *Superfast Formula 1 Racing*. Minneapolis: Lerner Publications, 2020.

Rule, Heather. *GOATs of Auto Racing*. Minneapolis: Abdo Publishing, 2022.

Storm, Marysa. *Formula 1 Cars*. Mankato, MN: Black Rabbit Books, 2020.

NOTE TO EDUCATORS

Visit **www.focusreaders.com** to find lesson plans, activities, links, and other resources related to this title.

INDEX

Answer Key: 1. Answers will vary; **2.** Answers will vary; **3.** B; **4.** B